PONIES
& RIDING

BY
Toni Webber
ILLUSTRATED BY
Estelle Phillips

MACDONALD

First published 1979
Reprinted 1980

Macdonald Educational Ltd
Holywell House
Worship Street
London EC2A 2EN

©Macdonald Educational 1979

Adapted and published in
the United States by
Silver Burdett Company,
Morristown, N.J.
1980 Printing

ISBN 0-382-06436-4
Library of Congress
Catalog Card No. 80-50944

About this book

This book has been carefully planned to help you become an expert. Look for the special pages to find the information you need. **RECOGNITION** pages, with an **orange flash** in the top right-hand corner, contain all the essential information to know and remember. **PROJECT** pages, with a **grey border**, suggest some interesting ideas for things to do and make. At the end of the book there is a useful **REFERENCE** section.

Your own pony

Getting to know your pony
If you are lucky enough to own a pony, you are responsible for all its needs. The friendship between you will quickly grow. But even at a riding school, you may have the same pony each time you go. This will give you the chance to build up a special relationship with it.

Talk to the pony, giving it words of encouragement and praise. Don't be shy of stroking it or patting it. Try to visit it in its stable or field. Give it its feed if you get the chance. The pony should not just connect you with riding lessons.

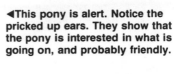
◀This pony is alert. Notice the pricked up ears. They show that the pony is interested in what is going on, and probably friendly.

▶Beware! This pony is not in the mood to be approached. Notice the ears, laid back flat. The eyes are also showing a lot of white.

◀This pony's ears are neither pricked up nor laid back. The eyelids are half-closed. The pony is relaxed, and may well be dozing.

How to tell a pony's mood

Get to know your pony's moods. The most obvious sign is the position of its ears. You should always watch the ears when you approach a strange pony.

If the ears are pricked, the pony is interested and probably friendly.

If the ears are laid flat back, this may be a warning that the pony is feeling uncomfortable and might bite or kick. This is especially true if the eyes are rolling and showing a lot of white.

If the ears are neither back nor forward, the pony is probably dozing, or at least feeling relaxed.

How the ears move

A pony can move its ears independently. For example, when its rider speaks to it, it may move one ear back, apparently in order to hear what is being said.

Looking after a pony

Feeding titbits

Ponies tend to be rather greedy. If they are constantly fed titbits, they may become bad-tempered when titbits aren't offered. This is especially true of very young ponies. A wise rider only gives titbits as a reward for good behaviour: **after** a ride, for example.

Give slices of apple or carrot. They should be cut in finger-shaped slices, so they cannot stick in the pony's throat. Only give sugar lumps sparingly.

Place the titbit in the palm of your hand. Keep the hand flat, with the fingers stretched out and together. Tuck your thumb out of the way, and let the pony take the titbit with its lips.

Always place titbits on the palm of your hand.

Lead a pony along the road unless it is safe in traffic.

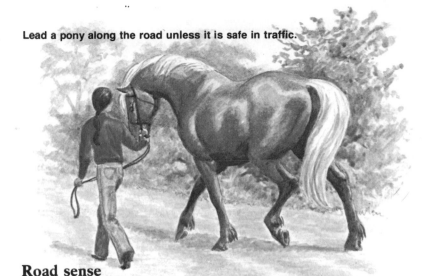

Road sense

Never ride a pony on the road unless you know it is
safe in traffic. Keep to the left. Walk along the grass
verge if there is one, but never ride on the
pavement. A group of riders should always go in
single file.

Always ride on a short rein and never go faster
than a slow trot. If you would like a driver to slow
down, wave an outstretched arm up and down.
Thank the driver afterwards.

☐   Always use bridleways if you can. These are
rights of way for riders to cross other people's land.
☐   If there are no bridleways, try to keep to clearly
defined tracks. If possible, obtain permission before
entering private property.
☐   Leave all gates as you find them.
☐   Keep to the edges of fields with crops in them.
☐   Never enter fields with farm animals in them.
☐   If told you are trespassing, apologize and turn
back.

The points of a horse

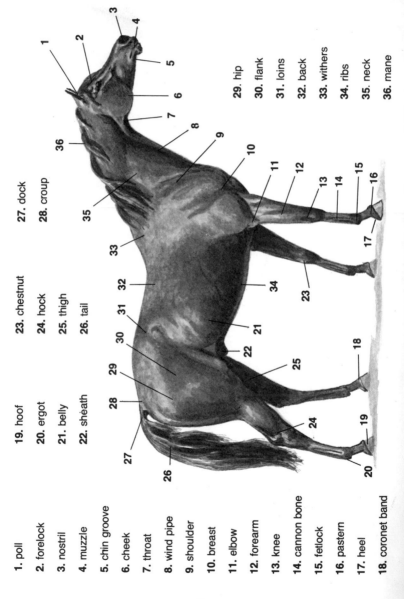

1. poll
2. forelock
3. nostril
4. muzzle
5. chin groove
6. cheek
7. throat
8. wind pipe
9. shoulder
10. breast
11. elbow
12. forearm
13. knee
14. cannon bone
15. fetlock
16. pastern
17. heel
18. coronet band

19. hoof
20. ergot
21. belly
22. sheath
23. chestnut
24. hock
25. thigh
26. tail
27. dock
28. croup
29. hip
30. flank
31. loins
32. back
33. withers
34. ribs
35. neck
36. mane

Face markings

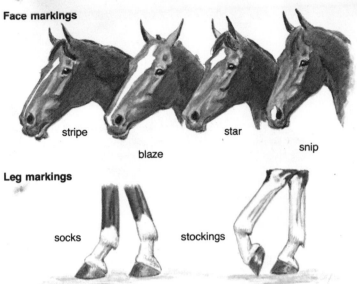

stripe

blaze

star

snip

Leg markings

socks

stockings

Horse and pony colours

chestnut

grey

bay

black

cream

roan

dun

skewbald

piebald

How to draw horses

Using a grid
You can use the scale drawing shown below as a guide to the proportions of a pony. The sides of each square are the same size as the length of the pony's head.

Notice that the body is basically three 'heads' long and three 'heads' high.

Draw a similar grid, using whatever measurement you like for the head length (2 cm or 5 cm for example).

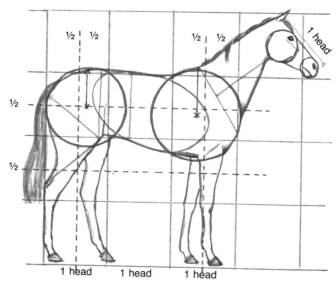

½ | ½   ½ | ½   1 head

½

½

1 head   1 head   1 head

The basic body shape
Now you have seen the proportions using the grid method, try drawing freehand.

The main thing to remember is that the horse's body is a series of ovals and circles. Try to see it in terms of these curved shapes, and build up the body bit by bit. Notice the use of ovals and circles on the facing page.

The body oval
This is the first thing you should draw. Next, add circles at the front and rear of the body oval, as shown opposite.

part of the gallop

standing still

cropping grass

the rear view

Drawing the head
Heads are particularly tricky. Remember the circles and ovals. Notice the position of the eyes: quite high on the head. Notice how triangles can be used to build up the full-face view.

side view

full-face view

What to wear

Riding clothes should be comfortable, practical and neat. The girl on the left is wearing casual clothes. The boy on the right is wearing smarter clothes suitable for almost any occasion: a Pony Club rally, a hunter trial or a meet. Both are wearing hard hats which are essential protective headgear.

Casual clothes

hard hat

shoes with heel

Casual clothes
Jeans are fine for short rides and dirty jobs such as cleaning out stables. For longer rides, wear jodhpurs. Jeans will chafe your legs.

Polo-neck jumpers are warm, and anoraks give good protection.

If you have long hair, keep it tied back to stop it blowing in your eyes.

Safety
Always wear a hard hat. And always wear one with a chin strap (cloth or elastic) to keep it on your head.

Shoes or boots should have a heel. Avoid wide shoes and shoes with buckles. They could get stuck in the stirrups.

Smarter wear

For smarter occasions you can wear a plain shirt and tie, tweed jacket, stretch jodhpurs and jodhpur boots. String gloves are useful on a wet day. They stop your hands slipping on the reins.

Never wear a black jacket for hacking. Black jackets are for hunting and showing.

Hard hat

This should always be worn with the peak pulled well down over your forehead.

chin strap

Hacking jacket

This should be worn with a white shirt and a tie. In wet weather, a riding mac is useful. String gloves will stop the reins from slipping through your fingers.

crop

Jodhpurs

These are reinforced on the inside of the knee to stop the stirrup leathers from rubbing.

Boots

Can be made of leather or rubber. Lace-up shoes with a heel are also fine for riding. But never wear slip-on shoes or wellingtons as they can easily get caught in the stirrups.

13

Tacking up

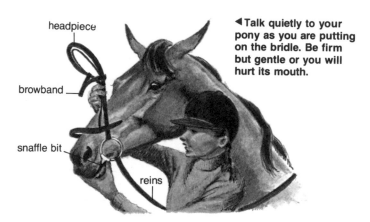

headpiece

browband

snaffle bit

reins

◄ **Talk quietly to your pony as you are putting on the bridle. Be firm but gentle or you will hurt its mouth.**

Putting on the bridle
1. Hold the bridle in your left hand. Use the right to slip the rein over the pony's head.

Put your arm under the pony's neck. Grasp the bridle just below the browband with your right hand, supporting the weight of the bit with your left.

2. Raise the bridle so that you can guide the bit into the pony's mouth with your left hand.

If it won't open its mouth, insert your thumb into the corner, then gently push in the bit. (There are no teeth here, so you won't get bitten.)

headpiece

When you have put on the bridle, lift the pony's forelock over the top of the browband.

3. As the bit enters its mouth, transfer your left hand to the headpiece and ease the bridle over the pony's ears.

Do up the throatlash and noseband. Check that all loose ends are through their keepers.

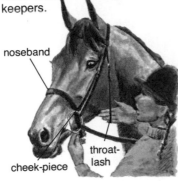

noseband

cheek-piece

throat-lash

Untacking
Undo the throatlash and noseband. Take the buckle end of the rein in your right hand. Bring it up to the headpiece. Hold the rein and headpiece together in both hands. Slip the bridle over the ears.

(To untack the saddle, run up the stirrups and undo the girth. Take the saddle in both hands. Remove it in one backwards movement, switching it to one arm and catching up the girth.)

◄**The cheek-pieces hold the bit at the correct height. Make sure that they are level on each side.**

Putting on the saddle
1. See that the stirrup irons are run up the leathers and that the girth is folded back over the seat. Take the saddle in both hands and lift it onto the pony's back.

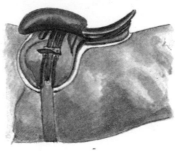

Bring it down gently, so it is well forward on the withers. Slide it back into position. Go round to the other side and unfold the girth.

2. Check that the buckles are done up and the girth is not twisted. Return to the near side and bring the girth round under the belly. Fasten the buckles on the near side.

At first, don't do the girth up too tightly. But check the tightness when you are mounted. The saddle should be held firmly in position, but not so tight that the pony is uncomfortable.

Mounting

Before you try to mount your pony, make sure it is standing quite still. Avoid rough, jerky movements as you get up. These may startle the pony and cause it to shift position, making mounting much harder.

Remember the same principles when you dismount. Your pony should be standing absolutely still before you begin to get down.

positioning the left foot

Grasp the saddle with both hands, as shown below. Now pivot on your right foot and spring lightly upwards.

ready to mount

Mounting
Stand with your left shoulder nearest the pony's left shoulder, facing the tail.

Pick up the reins by the buckle. Gather both sides together in your left hand, just in front of the saddle, as shown above.

Place your left foot in the stirrup iron, guiding it in with your right hand. Steady yourself with your left hand if necessary.

Swing your right leg over the back of the saddle, moving your right hand to the front of the saddle at the same time.

Lower yourself gently into position.

springing into the saddle

Slip your right foot into the stirrup iron and take up the reins in both hands. Check the girth and stirrups and then move off.

swinging the right leg over

Dismounting

Bring the pony to a halt. Take your feet out of the stirrups.

Lean forwards with both hands on the pommel of the saddle, while still keeping hold of the reins for control.

Now swing your right leg over the back of the saddle, as in the illustration above. Drop lightly to the ground.

The reins should still be in your hand, and you should be pointing forwards when you land.

Mounting and dismounting are normally carried out from the near (left) side of the horse. But it is a good idea to practise from both sides. Wrong-side mounting and dismounting may come in useful in gymkhanas.

How to ride

▼How to hold the reins.

Holding the reins

Hold the reins in both hands so that they pass under the little finger, or between the third and little finger, of each hand.

Grasp the reins lightly between thumb and forefinger. Your knuckles should be facing forwards with the thumbs on top.

Your wrists should be flexible enough to allow contact with the pony's mouth while at the same time slightly following the movements of the head.

Sitting position

Sit centrally in the deepest part of the saddle. Adjust your stirrup leathers so that your thighs lie lightly against the saddle. Your calves should rest comfortably against the pony's sides. Place the ball of the foot on the stirrup iron.

Keep your shoulders, hips and heels in a vertical line. Your hands should be level, one on either side of the pony's neck, just in front of the saddle. Keep your elbows tucked in close to your sides.

▲ The position of the leg and foot.

The correct way to sit

If you are sitting properly, your shoulders, hips and heels should form a straight line.

There are two kinds of aids to help you control your pony: natural aids and artificial aids.

Natural aids

These are your hands, legs, body and voice. You use all of these to tell your pony what to do. Your hands guide the pony by the reins. Your legs make it go forward and control its hindquarters. Your body weight is used to balance the pony. Your voice encourages it.

Artificial aids

These are the whip, spurs and martingale. The whip and spurs can be used at the same time as you do your leg actions. But you should only use them if you are an experienced rider. The martingale is a special attachment between the bridle and girth. It helps keep the pony's head under control.

A horse's paces

▲The walk

When your pony walks, he lifts each foot separately. Starting with the near hind foot, the other feet follow in order:
1. near hind
2. near fore
3. off hind
4. off fore

This sequence is known as a pace of **four-time**.

You should keep the position described on page 18, with head held high and eyes straight ahead. But your hands and body should move slightly in response to the horse's movement.

▲The trot

Here, your pony's legs move in pairs:
1. near fore and off hind together (the left diagonal)
2. off fore and near hind together (the right diagonal)

This is known as a pace of **two-time.**

Two-time is a very active pace. The rider must learn to rise from the saddle as one diagonal hits the ground, and sit back as the other comes down.

Once you have learned the rising trot (or 'posting'), you will never forget it—but it takes a lot of practice.

Horses and ponies have four basic paces: the walk, the trot, the canter and the gallop. For comfortable riding each one needs a different technique. Though it may take a little practice, it is worth learning how to ride correctly at each pace.

▲The canter
This has a pace of **three-time:**
1. near hind
2. near fore and off-hind together
3. off fore

At the canter, the legs on one side of the pony are always in front of the other two.

This is quite noticeable if you watch a pony cantering.

To be properly balanced your pony should canter in a circle, with the inside leg leading.

You should sit well down in the saddle. Your hands and body should follow the rhythm of the pony as it canters along.

▲The gallop
The gallop is simply a fast canter. The feet fall in the same sequence as in the canter. However, there is one moment when all four feet are off the ground at the same time. So the gallop is known as a pace of **four-time.**

When galloping, you should not allow your weight to fall on the pony's back. Lean forwards and raise yourself just clear of the saddle.

Your back should be straight, your head up and your shoulders forward. Support your weight with your knees and feet.

Exercises
to make you supple

To improve your balance, practise a few exercises every time you go for a ride. Ask a friend to hold the pony's head to make sure it does not move off while you are doing them. Fold the stirrups over the front of the saddle and drop the reins on to the pony's neck before you begin.

'round-the-world'

half-dismount

Round-the-world
Lift your right leg over the pommel and twist round in the saddle. Lift your left leg over the back so that you are sitting facing the tail.

Continue 'round the world' until you are back in the right position.

Repeat the exercise three times in both directions.

Half-dismount
Start as for 'round-the-world'. But when both legs are on the same side, twist so that you can grasp the front and back of the saddle with your hands.

Balance there for a moment, legs dangling. Then swing your right leg over the back of the saddle and return to the sitting position. Repeat two or three times on both sides.

Scissors

Lean forward and put your hands on the pony's neck. Swing both legs back and upwards, supporting your weight on your hands.

When your legs rise above the pony's quarters, cross them, twist, and sit up facing the pony's tail.

Repeat the exercise with your hands on the pony's quarters to get back to the right position.

This is quite a difficult exercise, and you may need a helper to make sure that you don't fall off. To make it more fun, why not have races with your friends?

scissors

rising from the saddle

arm-circling

Back, thighs and arms

By stretching your legs down and your head up repeatedly, you will make your back supple.

Strengthen your thighs by straightening your legs in the stirrups and lifting your seat from the saddle.

Swinging and circling your arms will make them stronger.

How to feed your pony

quick-release knot

How often should you feed your pony?
In the wild, ponies spend a lot of time grazing. They have very small stomachs for their size, so they eat 'little and often'. When feeding your pony, you should apply the same principle.

In the summer months when grass is growing it is very nutritious. Your pony will need little else.

In winter, replace grass with hay. The hay should not be too rich. Choose meadow or seed hay. It is best between six and 18 months old.

A hay net

To avoid waste, feed hay to your pony in a hay net, tied with a quick-release knot (see opposite). Make sure it does not dangle on the ground where the pony might trip over it.

Energy foods

If you work your pony hard, it will need extra food for energy, such as pony nuts or oats. These are called concentrates. But don't give oats to a small pony. They will make it over-excited and unmanageable.

Mix concentrates with broad bran and chaff (chopped hay). Dried sugar beet, soaked in water overnight, and boiled barley will help a thin pony to put on weight. Carrots and turnips are other good energy foods.

Finally, remember to give your pony lots of water every day and make sure you exercise it, or it may get a painful disease of the feet, called *laminitis*.

Feeding calendar for a pony at grass		
Month	**Hay**	**Concentrates**
January	Yes	If necessary
February	Yes	If necessary
March	Yes	If necessary
April	Yes	If necessary
May	No	No
June	No	No
July	No	No
August	No	If necessary during holidays
September	No	No
October	Yes	No
November	Yes	No
December	Yes	If necessary

Keeping a pony in a field

A pony's field should have secure fencing and gate, shelter and an ample supply of fresh water. About 1½ to 2 acres per pony is ideal. Check the field to make sure it contains no poisonous plants.

Post and rail fencing is best, though post and wire is cheaper and quite adequate. Avoid barbed wire.

A high hedge or hollow make good windbreaks and trees give shade. If the field has none of these you will need a field shelter or three-sided shed.

A clear running stream gives the best supply of fresh water. But you can also use mains water to supply an automatic trough, or just fill a water trough by hose. Check the water level every day and clean out the trough four times a year. In winter, break the ice at least once a day. An adequate water supply is essential.

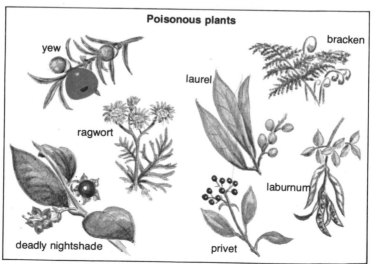

Poisonous plants

yew

bracken

laurel

ragwort

laburnum

deadly nightshade

privet

If you keep your pony in a field, make sure he has everything he needs.

field shelter

strong fence

water trough

tree for shade

stream

plenty of grass

Catching your pony

When you go to catch your pony, never rush at it. If necessary, tempt it with titbits in a bucket while you put the halter on. If it is hard to catch, try leaving it in the field with its headcollar on. Try also catching it when you don't intend to ride it. Just make a great fuss of it, then let it go again.

Bridles and bits

headpiece

browband

cavesson noseband

throatlash

cheek-piece

snaffle bit

The parts of a bridle

reins

Bits

Bits are pieces of metal which pass through the pony's mouth, over its tongue. There are lots of different types, but all are variations of three basic designs: snaffle, curb and pelham.

Snaffle: has a ring at each end to which bridle and reins are attached. The mouthpiece is usually jointed, and may be plain or twisted.

Curb: can be straight, curved or hooped with shanks on each side.

Pelham: like the curb but with extra rings at the top of the shanks for the snaffle rein.

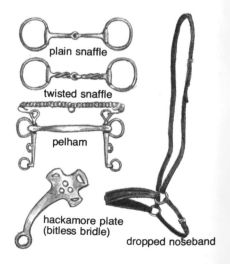

plain snaffle

twisted snaffle

pelham

hackamore plate
(bitless bridle)

dropped noseband

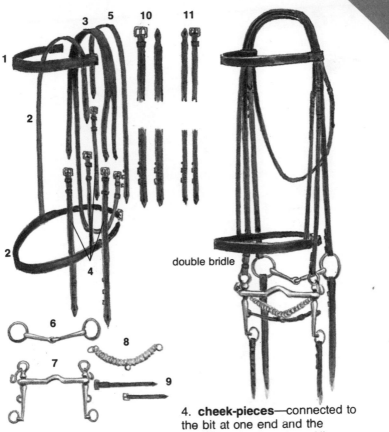

double bridle

The bridle

A bridle is made up of various pieces of leather which keep the bit in the correct position in the pony's mouth.

Parts of the bridle

1. **browband**—lies below the ears and stops the headpiece from slipping back.
2. **noseband**—called a cavesson. Is mainly decorative. Only used to attach a standing martingale
3. **headpiece**—passes over the pony's head behind the ears.

4. **cheek-pieces**—connected to the bit at one end and the headpiece at the other. Allows the height of the bit to be adjusted.
5. **bridoon cheek and sliphead.**
6. **bridoon snaffle bit.**
7. **Weymouth curb bit.**
8. **curb chain.**
9. **lip strap.**
10. **snaffle reins.**
11. **curb reins.**
12. **throatlash** (see picture opposite) — strap of the headpiece which buckles under the pony's throat and prevents the bridle from slipping off.

Saddles

What to look for
A good saddle should be comfortable for both pony and rider. It should be the right size, and properly padded so that no part of it rests on the pony's spine. In a good saddle, the stuffing underneath spreads the weight of the rider over the fleshy parts of the pony's back.

Which saddle to buy?
A general purpose saddle or a 'Pony Club Approved' saddle are best if your riding consists mainly of hacking, with perhaps a little show-jumping and gymkhana work. They both have a fairly deep seat. The flap and panel are cut less far forward than those on a jumping saddle. The front edge of the panel may also have a knee roll.

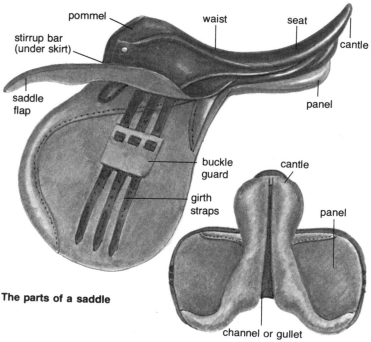

pommel

waist

seat

cantle

stirrup bar
(under skirt)

saddle
flap

panel

buckle
guard

cantle

girth
straps

panel

The parts of a saddle

channel or gullet

jumping saddle

knee roll

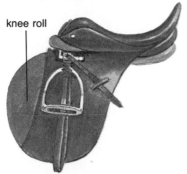

▲Jumping saddle
This has an exaggerated forward cut and sturdy knee rolls for extra support.

▼Side saddle
The side saddle allows the rider to sit with both legs on the same side of the horse. It has a flat seat and one stirrup for the left foot. It is rarely used today except for showing.

side saddle

pad saddle or 'numnah'   crupper

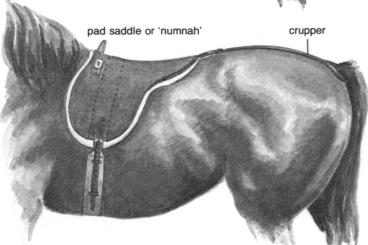

▲Pad saddle
This is a simple saddle-shaped felt pad. It rarely has a tree or framework. It is worn by donkeys and ponies which are too small for an ordinary saddle.

A pad saddle is usually fitted with a crupper. This is a strap which is looped round the pony's tail and attached to the back of the saddle. It stops the saddle from slipping forward.

Keeping a pony in a stable

The stable

It should be at least 3 metres square for a 12.2 h.h. pony. Then, when the pony rolls, it won't get 'cast' or jammed against the side of the box. The door should be wide (about 1.4 metres), split in two halves, with the top left open for ventilation.

The floor should be of non-porous concrete with a slight slope for drainage. You need a manger, a ring for the haynet, and a water bucket which should be kept full at all times.

Bedding

Use wood shavings, sawdust, peat or straw. Wheat makes the best straw bedding and should be shaken up to separate the stalks. Damp and dirty straw must be removed every morning and fresh straw put down.

Mucking out

Always muck out once a day – dirty straw will soon smell very unpleasant.

This pony is nibbling its owner's hair while she cleans out its stable: one of the hazards of working with horses!

holder for water bucket

Food and water

Food should consist of hay, greenstuff and concentrates. The concentrates should be fed three or four times a day. Keep the water bucket in a special holder to stop your pony from knocking it over.

haynet

rough concrete floor

33

The tack room

bridle hook

saddle rack

Saddles

These should be stored on shaped racks. Never throw a saddle on the ground, or the tree may break. If you have to put a saddle down for a moment, rest it on the pommel and flaps.

Bridles

Hang bridles up by the headpiece. Use bridle hooks or two nails about 5 cm apart. Make sure the reins don't trail on the ground. Stirrup leathers, irons and bits can be hung on nails by their buckles or rings.

Store feedstuffs in galvanized dustbins. You will also need a set of scales and scoops for measuring the pony's feed.

How to store your tack

Making a saddle rack
Use eleven lengths of wood, cut and nailed to the shape shown below. The two legs at each end should form triangles with the base.

Detail: cut each end to an angle like this. Nail to the centre crosspiece.

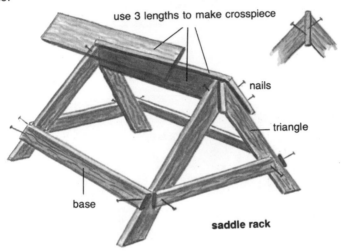

use 3 lengths to make crosspiece

nails

triangle

base

saddle rack

You will need four stretchers for solid support at the base. Make the crosspiece from three lengths joined as shown in the detail. Never store saddles on top of one another.

Bridle hooks
To make a bridle hook, first saw a section from a round log or thick branch. The section should be about 10 cm. in diameter.

Remove the bark and varnish the wood. Fix the bridle hook to the wall with a long, stout screw.

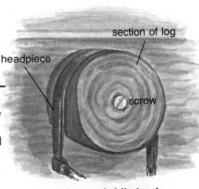

section of log

headpiece

screw

bridle hook

Grooming kit

Cleaning your tack
This should be done thoroughly at least once a week. Remove dirt from the leatherwork. Then, when the leather is dry, rub in saddle soap with a damp sponge (not too wet or the soap will foam). Brush cloth saddle-linings with a stiff brush.

Wash all metalwork in soapsuds. Dry it, clean it with metal polish and buff it with a soft cloth.

Grooming kit

dandy brush

Dandy brush
This stiff-bristled brush is for removing caked mud from the pony's neck and body. Don't use it on the pony's head. Use only lightly on its legs.

Body brush
This is a short, soft-bristled brush. It can be used on all parts of the pony, including the mane and tail. It is good for any sensitive areas.

body brush

Curry comb
This is used for cleaning the body brush. It can be made of metal, plastic or rubber.

curry comb

Mane comb
A stubby metal or plastic comb, used when plaiting or 'pulling' (thinning out) the mane and tail.

mane comb

Wisp and stable rubber
The wisp is for toning up the muscles. The rubber is for polishing the pony's coat.

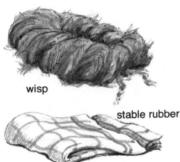

wisp

stable rubber

Water brush and sponge
These are used damp. The sponge is for wiping sensitive areas. The brush is for the mane, tail and hooves.

water brush

sponge

Hoof pick
This is a specially shaped hook for picking out stones and dirt from a pony's hooves.

Care of the feet
A pony's feet should be examined and cleaned out every day.

Stand close to the pony, facing the tail and run your hand down its leg. When the pony's weight shifts to the opposite leg, gently raise the foot. Work downwards, taking care not to hurt the sensitive sole nor the soft parts of the frog.

picking out the hooves

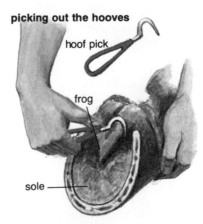

hoof pick

frog

sole

Grooming

Grooming a pony at grass

If your pony lives out, don't groom it too much. Otherwise you may remove the natural grease which keeps its coat warm and waterproof. Just brush mud from the coat and remove tangles from the mane and tail, and pick out the feet.

Grooming a stabled pony

A stabled pony needs more care. First pick out each foot. Then use the body brush, working from ears to tail. Don't forget the belly or the insides of the legs. Brush the mane and tail, separating the hairs. Clean the brush frequently with a curry comb.

Sponge the eyes, nostrils, lips and dock. Polish the coat with the stable rubber and lightly oil the outsides of the hooves with hoof oil.

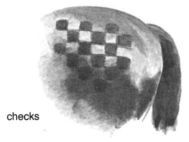

checks

maple leaf

Your pony will look especially smart for a show or gymkhana with one of these patterns on its quarters. Make them by brushing the hairs the wrong way. Use a short-bristled water brush, slightly dampened.

horseshoe

Improving the mane and tail

Plaiting the mane

Dampen the mane with a water brush. Divide it into sections with a mane comb. Now plait each section in turn.

Secure the ends with a needle and thread. Roll under so each plait forms a knot, snug against the crest. Bind and stitch the knot to keep it secure.

Always have an uneven number of plaits on the neck, plus one on the forelock.

Undo the plaits at the end of the day and brush the mane out.

Pulling the mane and tail

If the mane is too thick, pull out a few hairs at a time by the roots. Take them from the underside of the mane. Don't use scissors except behind the ears and in front of the withers.

unpulled

pulled

▼Tails can be pulled or plaited, then trimmed to 'bang' or 'switch' shapes.

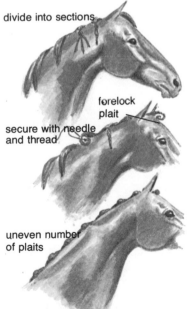

divide into sections

forelock plait

secure with needle and thread

uneven number of plaits

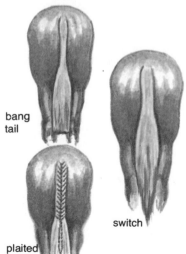

bang tail

switch

plaited

Protective clothing

Rugs

Rugs keep a clipped pony warm or help a sweating pony to dry off. There are many kinds, but all are shaped to cover a pony's shoulders, back and quarters. They buckle across the chest and are kept in place by a strap, called a surcingle.

This passes right round the body and fastens on the near side. If padded at the withers it is called a roller.

Anti-sweat rug
Made of open mesh to cool a sweating pony without giving it a chill.

Night rug with roller
Made of jute with a wool lining. In winter, it can be worn over a blanket if the nights are very cold.

New Zealand rug
Made of canvas with wool lining. Designed for a clipped pony when out in a field. The roller passes through slots on either side and there are leg straps at the rear.

Day rug and roller
Made of wool. Usually in plain colours. The roller holds the blanket on.

Summer sheet
Made of cool cotton. Keeps off dust and flies, and protects a pony from draughts.

Woollen underblanket
Often used in winter as extra protection against the cold.

The items below help protect a pony from injury, especially when travelling.

Tailguard and bandages
A felt tailguard is strapped round the tail and tied below the dock bone. Bandages also protect the tail and help keep the hair in position.

Hockboot
This is a special protective pad, made of leather. It is strapped around the hock joint when a pony is travelling, to prevent injury.

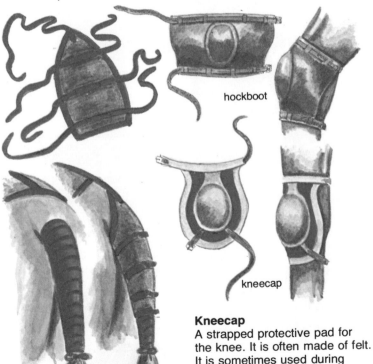

hockboot

kneecap

bandage   tailguard

Kneecap
A strapped protective pad for the knee. It is often made of felt. It is sometimes used during exercises when it must not be strapped on too tight in case it stops the flow of blood.

A visit to the blacksmith

The parts of the hoof

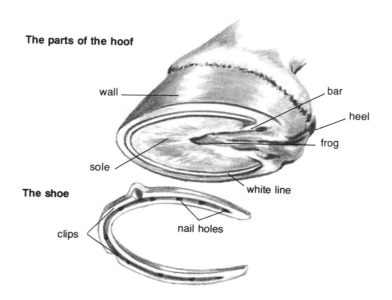

wall

bar

heel

frog

sole

white line

The shoe

clips

nail holes

Cold shoeing
A pony in normal work will probably need new shoes every six to eight weeks. For cold shoeing, the blacksmith measures the pony's feet, and returns to his forge to make the shoes.

Later, he removes the old shoes, trims the feet and nails the new shoes through the horny part of each hoof. He then twists off the pointed ends and hammers the 'clenches' (blunt ends) down.

Hot shoeing
For this, the pony is taken to the forge, where the farrier tries a red-hot shoe onto its hoof. He can then make adjustments while the metal is still soft; this method ensures the best fit.

The pony's hoof

The V-shaped **frog** underneath the foot acts as a shock absorber when the pony moves around. There are deep hollows on either side of it. These must be cleaned regularly to prevent infection.

The **sole** is very sensitive and can be bruised or pierced by a stone or thorn.

The horn of the **wall** grows downwards from the coronet. It grows quite quickly. Sometimes it has to be trimmed before the shoes are worn out.

Hot shoeing

A pony's age

Examining the teeth

Ponies grow milk teeth during their first year. In their third year, these begin to be replaced by permanent teeth. You can tell a pony's age by looking at its teeth. The pictures below will help you to recognize the different stages.

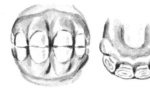

One-year-old: a full set of milk teeth has appeared.

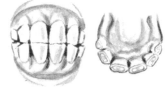

Three-year-old: two permanent teeth appear in the middle.

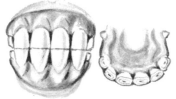

Five-year-old: all the milk teeth have been replaced by permanent teeth.

Seven-year-old: hooks appear on the back of the top corner teeth. They only last one year.

Eight-year-old: the hooks on the top corner teeth have disappeared. Now, telling the age becomes harder.

Fifteen-year-old: the corner teeth now have a line known as Galvayne's groove, reaching halfway down.

The age at which a pony should be ridden

Racehorses start their careers at two years old. But ponies mature much later. No pony should be broken in before it is four years old.

Buying a pony

A young pony is not strong enough to cope with all the activities that young riders like to take part in. If it is forced to carry a rider's weight when it is still little more than a baby itself, its back may be damaged. So you shouldn't buy a pony that is too young.

It is also important not to buy a pony that is too old. An old pony will not be able to manage a very full programme. It is, however, very safe for a beginner to learn on.

A horse that is too old to be ridden is often put out to grass.

Teaching your pony to jump

Practising with trotting poles.

Trotting over poles

Start by exercising your pony over trotting poles laid
on the ground. These teach your pony to adjust its
balance and stride. Just use one pole at first.

Walk over it a few times, always going straight
and turning properly afterwards. Then add a second
pole, about 1½ metres from the first. Walk quietly
over both. When your pony is stepping cleanly over
them without hesitation, add a third pole. Continue
until you have six poles at regular intervals. The
pony should trot over them confidently.

The first jump

Now add a proper jump. It should be very low: no
more than 45 cm high. Set it about 2½ metres from
the last trotting pole. The best jumps for these
training purposes are cavaletti (see page 50).

Your first jumps should be very low.

The right position for jumping

Shorten your leathers by two holes. Slide your hands forward as the pony takes off, and bend at the waist.

When the pony has learnt to come quietly to the first jump and keeps on going afterwards, add another low jump. It should be about 5 metres further on.

When to remove the trotting poles

Keep on exercising over the jumps. Add more as you progress, and vary the distance between them. When the pony is tackling them with confidence, take away the trotting poles one by one. By now the pony should be clearing the jumps in a balanced way.

The stages of a jump

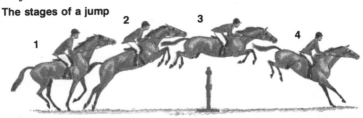

The four main stages of a jump are classified as:
1. approach; 2. take-off;
3. clearance; and 4. landing.

Keep your heels down and your seat just clear of the saddle. Your hands and forearms should form a straight line with the reins.

Types of jump

There are two basic types of show jump: the upright and the spread. The **spread** is usually big and impressive-looking. But the **upright** is often harder. It is tricky to judge the right moment for take-off. And because it looks easy the horse can get careless.

Uprights

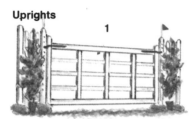

Gate: usually five-barred, but may be curved.

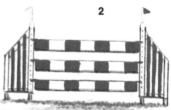

Planks: three or four on edge, sometimes with 'No Entry' sign.

Post and rails: normally has three or four rails.

Wall: looks fairly solid, which encourages the horse to jump.

Spread fences

Water jump: often has a low hedge in front, slanting towards the water.

Double oxer: a hedge with rails in front and behind. It is hard for a horse to jump cleanly.

The horse tends to see the hedge a lot more clearly than the rails in front of it.

Hog's back: a set of poles in the middle, with low poles on either side.

In most pole-jumps, the poles are held in metal cups and only fall if knocked very hard.

Triple bars: three poles placed in ascending order. These are easier to jump than the parallel poles because the pony can see each one quite clearly.

Parallel poles: two sets of rails parallel to one another. They are difficult to jump because the spread is at the highest point.

Building your own jumps

A set of show jumps is very expensive. It is only worth buying one if you are really keen on jumping. But you can make a good variety of jumps at home.

Cavaletti jumps

It is best to start with these because they are so useful for schooling purposes. Cavaletti are the jumps with X-shaped end-pieces.

Cavaletti

Each jump has two X-shaped end pieces. They are linked by a pole bolted into the top angle of each end piece.

Use stout timber for the end pieces. Carve a groove at the centre of each piece and slot them together. Cut angles at each end.

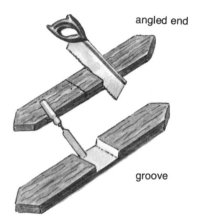

angled end

groove

Use a square pole for the cross-piece. Slant the edges to make it fit better. Nail it into the end pieces.

You can pile cavaletti on top of one another to give extra height and spread. The more cavaletti you make, the more varied jumps you can set up.

nail like this

Arranging your jumps

The pictures on the right show some of the ways in which you can use cavaletti.

You will see that the cross-piece does not have to lie on top. If you place a cavaletto on its side, the jump will be slightly lower. If you place it upside down, the jump will be lower still.

If you put three cavaletti in a row, it is a good idea to have the approach pole slightly lower than the others.

If you place one on top of two more, use the top cavaletto upside down at first, so the jump is not too hard.

Home-made wall

You will need enough wood to make two simple frames. They should be rectangular in shape and reinforced with stretchers in the middle. Stack one on top of the other and nail them together securely. Then cover the frame with canvas and paint it to look like bricks.

Adjustable pole jump

Make two X-shaped supports for the base. Choose two sturdy lengths of timber for the uprights. Drill holes in the uprights at regular intervals. These will take wooden dowels or pegs to carry the poles. Drill the holes at an angle so that the pegs slope upwards when in position.

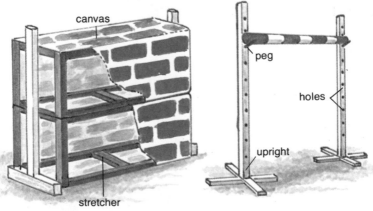

canvas

stretcher

peg

holes

upright

Gymkhanas

Racing for the winning-post!

Before the event

If you are taking part, exercise your pony only lightly the day before. Clean your tack thoroughly. If you are hacking to the gymkhana, give yourself plenty of time to get there.

When you arrive

First, untack your pony, put on its head collar and tie it up in the place allotted. Choose a shady spot if it is hot, and don't tie it too near other ponies in case they start to kick.

Make your way to the secretary's tent to collect your number. About half an hour before your event, tack up your pony and exercise it quietly in a corner. When you hear your event announced, go to the collecting ring and wait quietly for your turn.

Afterwards

Always accept the judge's decision without argument, and do find time to thank the organizers. If you are hacking home, ride your pony slowly. Walk the last kilometre to allow it to cool off.

Leading a pony into the ring.

Organizing your own gymkhana

Form a committee with friends. Decide on the date, and where the gymkhana is to be held (get permission if necessary).

Schedule of events
This should state the cost of entry for each class, the age limits, and the name and address of the secretary to whom entry forms must be sent. Distribute copies to your riding friends.

Things to remember
Collect all the equipment. Book a loudspeaker and appoint judges and stewards. Organize refreshments. Borrow a tent or trailer for the secretary to use.

Set up the gymkhana area, and a jump area if space is available. Suggestions for layout are shown on the facing page.

On the day
You will have quite enough to do running the show so it is best not to compete yourself.

Try to keep events running on time, and if there are delays explain the reasons over the loudspeaker.

When it is all over
Clear everything up and return all borrowed equipment. Don't forget to thank all those who have helped you.

Rosettes
It is very easy to make your own rosettes. Try to allow six for each class.

First, gather a piece of ribbon as shown in figure 1.

cardboard circle

Stitch the ends together. Then staple on another short length of ribbon (figure 2).

Finally, cut circles out of card, number them and glue them in position (figure 3).

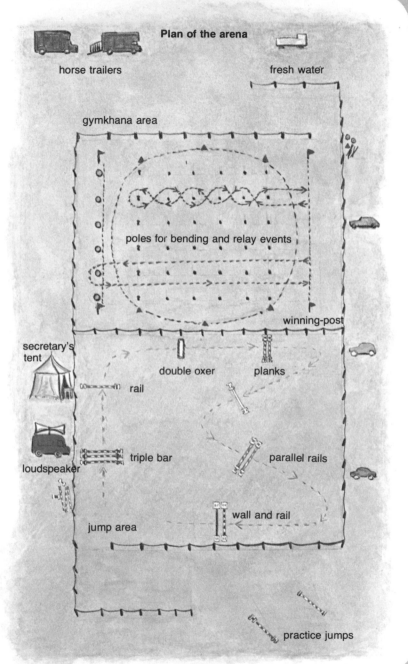

Plan of the arena

horse trailers

fresh water

gymkhana area

poles for bending and relay events

winning-post

secretary's tent

double oxer

planks

rail

loudspeaker

triple bar

parallel rails

wall and rail

jump area

practice jumps

Dressage

Dressage means schooling a horse or pony so that it becomes a better ride. Regular dressage exercises will help your pony to be a better show jumper, gymkhana performer or whatever else you enjoy. Dressage can also be an event in itself.

The aim is to improve your pony's suppleness and obedience. Dressage exercises encourage harmony between a horse and its rider. Some can be practised at home.

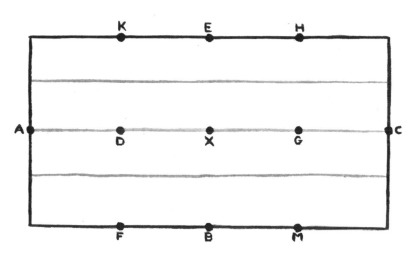

A dressage arena
The diagram above shows the layout of a suitable dressage arena. It should be 40 metres long by 20 metres wide, and laid out with lettered markers.

The diagram on the right shows one typical movement: **the serpentine**, executed between markers C, H, B, K and A.

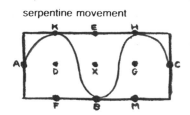

serpentine movement

▲A well-trained horse and rider.

Make your own dressage arena

You can buy lettered markers, which look a bit like traffic cones. Use them to mark out a practice arena in a field. Alternatively, you can use old paint tins, painted with the appropriate letters. Set them out as shown in the diagram on the left.

Don't try to do too much

You may want to try some of the movements you have seen in a dressage competition. But remember, the expert horse and rider have undergone a long period of training to achieve their perfect balance.

If you try to teach advanced movements to your pony, you will both end up completely confused. Concentrate instead on getting your pony to move forward freely and to be responsive to the aids you give him.

Reference section

Clubs and associations

The Pony Club

Anyone under 21 is eligible to join the Pony Club. It was founded in Great Britain in 1929 and now has branches all over the world.

The subscription at present is $6.00 a year. This entitles you to wear the Pony Club badge and tie and to attend meetings, camps and other activities organized by your local branch. You will also receive sound, practical advice on everything to do with ponies — so it is worth joining even if you don't have a pony of your own.

Meetings may be purely instructional or they can be fun affairs.

Some instructional meetings are for dismounted members only — teaching them, for example, how to clean out a stable properly.

Every member is expected to attend several of these instructional meetings per year. Not only are they enjoyable, they also prevent a rider from getting into bad habits.

If you ride at a riding school, you may find that it organizes Pony Club meetings for pupils who are Pony Club members. If so, you can hire a pony to ride during the rally from the school. Even when a meeting is held elsewhere, the school will usually allow you to hire a pony.

There are more than 327 groups in the United States so you are likely to find one in your area. If you have any problems, write to:

United States Pony Clubs
303 South High Street
West Chester, PA 19380

The 4-H Club

The 4-H Club would also be a good organization to get involved in if you are interested in ponies and horses. In addition to organizing animal husbandry projects, many groups also hold horse shows. For information write:

4-H Program
Extension Service
U.S. Dept. of Agriculture
Washington, DC 20250

The American Horse Shows Association

This organization promotes interest in horse shows, establishes and enforces rules governing horse shows, maintains records, sponsors junior competitions, and presents Horse of the Year Awards.

American Horse Shows
Association
598 Madison Avenue
New York, NY 10022

The National Riding Committee

The membership of this group consists of riders who have passed the rating test for riders as established by the committee. They encourage educated horseback riding through clinics, rating centers, seminars and competitions. They also maintain a job placement center for rated riders.

National Riding
Committee
% National Association
for Girls and Women
in Sport
2101 16th St. NW
Washington, DC 20036

U.S. Dressage Federation

The purpose of this group is to promote and encourage a high standard of accomplishment in dressage throughout the U.S., mostly through educational programs, and to improve the general understanding of dressage through clinics, forums and seminars.

U.S. Dressage Federation
P.O. Box 80668
Lincoln, NE 68501

Professional Horsemen's Association of America

The members of this group are professional, amateur and junior horsemen. The group sponsors horse shows, forums, and various social activities.

Professional Horsemen's
Association of America
301 N. Union Street
Kennett Square, PA
19348

Pony Breed Societies

Many breeds of ponies have their own societies. Each maintains a stud registry and pedigree records. Many hold clinics and horse shows. For information write to one of the groups below:

American Connemara Pony Society
HoshieKon Farm, R.D. 1
Goshen, CT 06756

American Shetland Pony Society
P.O. Box 435
Fowler, IN 47944

National Appaloosa Pony, Inc.
Box 206
Gaston, IN 47342

Pony of the Americas Club
P.O. Box 1447
Mason City, IA 50401

Welsh Pony Society of America
% V. Gail Headley
White Post, VA 22611

Horse Shows

Horse riders and horses from many lands compete in international horse shows. The practice of showing horses in competition has existed for many centuries. The Olympic Games and the medieval tournaments of England and Europe were early examples of our present-day horse shows. In the United States, the rodeo is in itself a type of horse show.

Most of the important horse shows in the United States are part of a national organization known as the *American Horse Shows Association* (A.H.S.A.), whose 50 directors represent every area and every type of horse.

Recognized horse shows exist in every state in the Union. The National Horse Show in New York City ranks as the largest annual horse event in the United States. It was first held in 1883. Several hundred non-recognized shows which operate separately from the A.H.S.A. are held annually too. For the most part they are one-day events.

Local horsemen's clubs also hold shows. Horses and their riders compete in many events such as jumping and the performance of various gaits. Other contests demonstrate the skill of harness horses and their drivers. Each such show makes its own individual rules and writes its own specifications for classes, not necessarily in agreement with the A.H.S.A. Rule Book. At these non-recognized events the winnings do not count as points toward the national championships offered by the A.H.S.A.

A horse show may be run either to raise funds for charitable purposes or simply in the interest of the sport. The participants are termed "exhibitors" and may enjoy either professional or amateur status. A professional is a person who earns his or her living in connection with horses. A precise rule defines an amateur.

During the riding season the clubs themselves organize competitions, which are called rallies. Rallies are always run on a team rather than on an individual basis. This means that riders learn to work together and help each other. Hard working members may have the chance to compete against teams from different clubs at regional and national rallies. It's a great thing to belong to a team and perhaps help your club win.

Glossary

Dorsal stripe: black or brown stripe down the backbone.

Filly: young female horse under four years old.

Foal: young pony less than one year old.

Fresh: a pony which is excitable because it needs exercise.

Full mouth: pony with all its second teeth.

Gait: a horse's pace.

Gall: a sore, usually caused by chafing. Saddle and girth galls are the most common types.

Gelding: a castrated male horse.

Groom: to clean and care for a pony or horse.

Hack: a lightweight riding hose.

Hackamore: bitless bridle.

Hand: measurement for describing the height of a horse. A hand is 10 cm.

Jog: a short-paced trot.

Lozenge: circular leather disc which fits between the bit ring and the horse's

Aged: horse or pony more than eight years old.

Amble: an artificial pace in which both legs on the same side move forward together.

Bars: part of the horse's mouth where there are no teeth. This is where the bit rests.

Bearing rein: rein on a harness horse which forces it to arch its neck.

Bridoon: the snaffle bit on a double bridle.

Broken knee: cut or graze to the knee of a pony.

Brood mare: mare used for breeding.

Cavesson: a leather noseband.

Colic: a bad stomach-ache.

Colt: a young male horse.

Dam: the mother of a horse or pony.

Dock: the root of the tail.

mouth, usually to prevent a sore from forming.

Lunge: to make a pony walk in a wide circle around a handler who controls it by means of a long rein.

Manege: the art of training and riding horses.

Mare: female horse or pony, aged four or more.

Paddock: a field or pasture used for keeping horses.

Rein back: to make a pony take a few steps backwards.

Roached mane: a mane clipped short.

Salt lick: lump of rock salt or special salt which is placed in a field or stable for a pony to lick.

Shy: the action of jumping sideways when a pony is frightened of something.

Sire: the father of a horse or pony.

Wall eye: bluish eye with a white surround. It does not affect the pony's sight.

Yearling: young horse or pony between the ages of one and two.

Booklist

If you want to learn more about riding and pony care, some of the publications listed below may be helpful. Also, look at the selection in your local library.

Horses and Ponies: Their Breeding, Feeding and Management by Marguerite De Beaumont (Sporting Book Center, Inc.)

Horses and Riding by Friederike Von Rokitansky (Dreenan Press, Inc.)

Horses and Riding by Betty Skelton (Hutchinson Merrimack Book Service)

Horses: Care, Riding, Jumping for All Ages by Robert Owen (Arco Publishing)

Horseshow Organization by L.C. Cooper (Sporting Book Center, Inc.)

Horseman's Manual by C.E. Hope (Charles Scribner's Sons)

Horses and Jumping by Ingvar Fredericson (Arco Publishing)

Horses and Horsemanship by M.E. Ensminger (Interstate)

Horses and Horse Shows by Harlan C. Abbey (A.S. Barnes)

Magazines

Horse and Rider *(monthly)*

Horse Lover's National Magazine *(bi-monthly)*

Horseman *(monthly)*

Index